ECO JOURNEYS

LIFE CYCLE OF A GLASS JAR

By Louise Nelson

BookLife
PUBLISHING

ISBN: 978-1-83927-856-3

Written by:
Louise Nelson

Edited by:
William Anthony

Designed by:
Dan Scase

©2021
BookLife Publishing Ltd.
King's Lynn
Norfolk PE30 4LS

A catalogue record for
this book is available
from the British Library.

Photo credits

Front cover – grafvision, Monkey Business Images, kim chul hyun. 4&5 – Tekkol, Kichigin. 6&7 – Ivaschenko Roman, DyziO. 8&9 – Africa Studio, dugwy39. 10&11 – vchal, mountainpix. 12&13 – Fotografiche, Evan Lorne. 14&15 – Photographee.eu, AVAVA, TeeStocker, Phovoir, rodimov. 16&17 – Somnuek saelim, Anton Kurashenko. 18&19 – Nataliia Yankovets, Atiketta Sangasaeng, ryby, roundex, Alter-ego, Somboon Bunproy, krasky, Africa Studio. 20&21 – Olga Madlewska, HollyHarry, Sharomka, Akhmad Dody Firmansyah, photosync. 22&23 – KAMPIAN CHENRAM, Andrii Spy_k, myboys.me, yalayama, Benoit Daoust. Images are courtesy of Shutterstock.com. With thanks to Getty Images, Thinkstock Photo and iStockphoto. All facts, statistics, web addresses and URLs in this book were verified as valid and accurate at time of writing. No responsibility for any changes to external websites or references can be accepted by either the author or publisher.

Contents

Words that look like this can be found in the glossary on page 24.

The Life of a Glass Jar

Glass jars are useful <u>containers</u>. Maybe you've seen them in the shops, full of jam or marmalade? Large jars are useful for keeping pasta, rice and flour in.

When they are empty, glass jars can be washed and used again. They can be reused in this way for a long time.

But what happens to glass jars when you are finally finished with them?

5

What IS Glass?

Glass is a material. A material is what an object is made of. The properties of a material tell us what it is like. Let's look at the properties of glass:

- Hard
- See-through
- Shiny
- Smooth
- Easily broken

We can see the jam inside the jar because the glass is see-through.

Glass is made of sand, which is <u>melted</u> until it is runny. Then it can be shaped into a bottle, jar or even a window! To melt sand, you must make it very hot, and this uses a lot of <u>energy</u>.

We should try and make less new glass. This will save energy and help the planet.

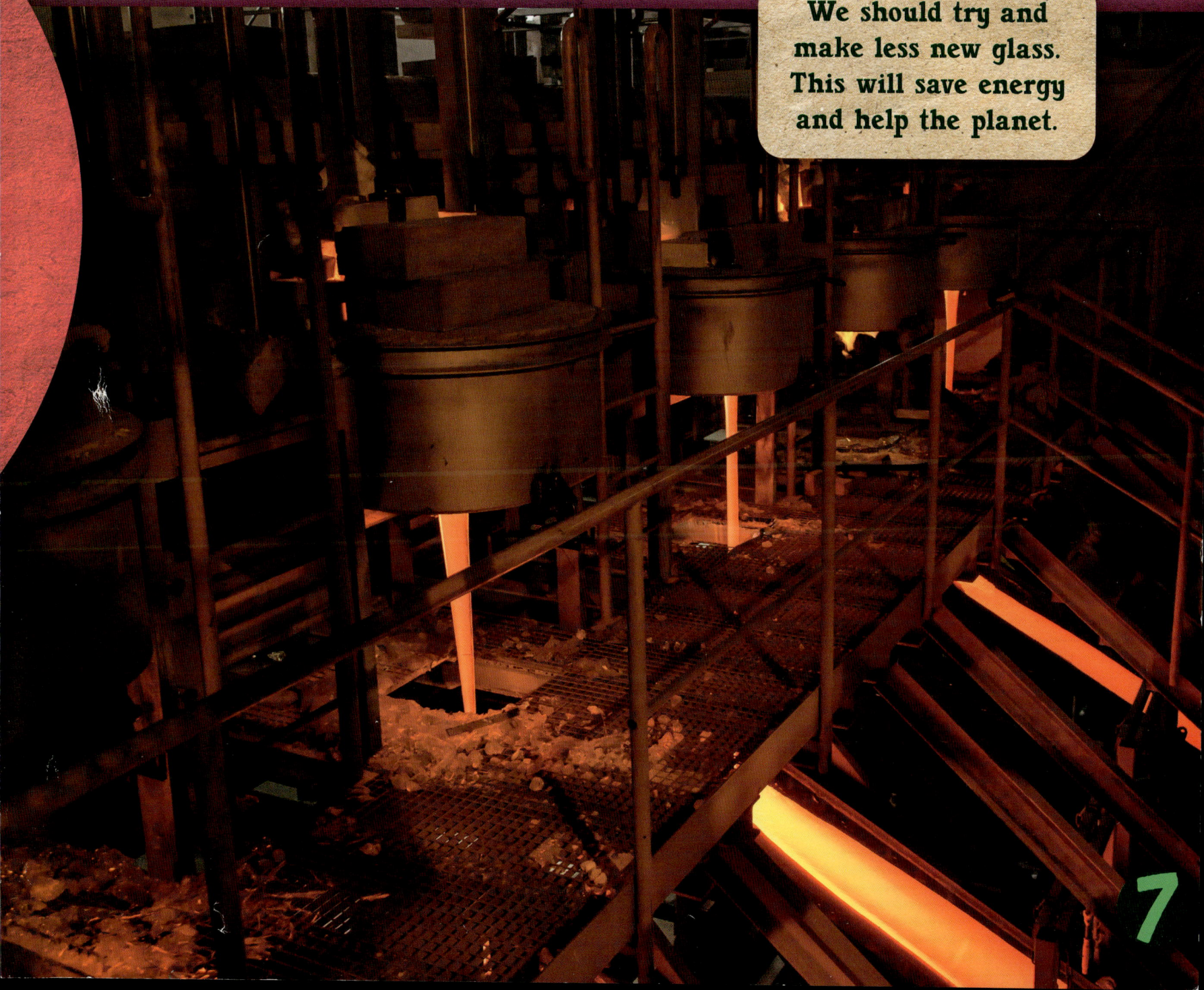

The Lifespan of a Glass Jar

Glass jars are very useful and can be used again and again. Glass is <u>waterproof</u> and will stay in the same shape – unless it is dropped, of course!

Broken glass is very sharp. Never touch it – always get an adult.

If you have too many glass jars and bottles, you might not be able to use them all. So what should you do with them when you are done?

Glass comes in lots of colours.

9

Glass Jars in Landfill

When we throw things into the bin, they are taken to landfill sites. These are areas where rubbish is put into the ground. Landfill sites are bad for the planet and <u>pollute</u> the land nearby.

Things in landfill break down and fall apart. Some materials break down slowly and others break down quickly. Glass stays in landfill for a very long time because it does not break down easily.

This glass vase was made thousands of years ago in ancient Rome.

What IS Recycling?

There are some materials you don't need to throw away when you are finished with them. Materials such as glass, paper, plastic and metal can be remade into something new. This is called recycling.

Glass can be recycled over and over again, forever. It can be melted and reshaped into new things, such as new jars, bottles and windows.

It is much easier to recycle glass than make new glass.

13

Recycling a Glass Jar

When you are finished with your glass jar, you must wash it to remove any food, glue or paint. You should also take off the lid and remove the label.

Metal and plastic lids can usually be recycled too.

If you have a recycling bin in your home, you can put the jar in there and it will be taken away to a recycling centre. If you don't have one, you can take your glass to a <u>public</u> recycling point.

At school

You can recycle glass in these places:

At home

This symbol means this bin is for recycling.

Out and about

At a recycling point

15

Inside a Recycling Centre

When the glass has been collected, it is taken to a recycling centre. Glass is <u>sorted</u> by type and colour, then smashed into small pieces. This smashed glass is called cullet.

Cullet

The cullet is ready to be recycled.

The cullet is melted and new glass is made. This new glass is formed into new bottles, jars and other items, ready to be filled and used again.

Trash to Treasure

When your glass jar has been recycled, it will have a new life as part of another object. Here are some things your jar could become!

Drinks glasses

A candle pot

Marbles

Glass beads

A glass lampshade

A new jar

A glass teacup

A glass vase

A cool piece of art

Most things made of glass have some recycled glass in them.

Reuse and Upcycle

When your jam jar is empty, you don't have to throw it away or recycle it. You can reuse it as something else.

Jars can be used to store all sorts of things, such as pencils, beads and paint brushes.

Upcycling means taking something old and used and making it look brand new. Could your jar become a vase, a lantern, or even a snow globe? Let's try upcycling a jar and see what we can make!

A lantern for Halloween

A money bank

A toothbrush holder

A festive decoration

The Eco Journey of a Glass Jar

The glass is turned into something new.

Glass is sorted and melted at the recycling centre.

The new jar is bought and used.

The jar is sent for recycling.

When it's empty, it must be washed and cleaned.

Quick Quiz

Can you remember the eco journey of a glass jar? Let's see! Look back through the book if you can't remember.

1. What is glass made from?
a) Melted sand
b) Crushed sand
c) Wet sand

2. What is crushed glass ready for recycling called?
a) Crumpet
b) Cullet
c) Custard

3. How many times can glass be recycled?
a) Once
b) Ten times
c) Over and over again

4. What does this symbol mean?
a) This bin is for glass only
b) This bin is for all recycling
c) This bin is for landfill

23

ANSWERS: 1) A, 2) B, 3) C, 4) B

Glossary

containers	things that other things can be put in
energy	a type of power that can be used to do something
melted	to be made runny like water, because of warm temperatures
pollute	make harmful or dirty through the actions of humans
public	open to people in the community
sorted	put into groups
waterproof	water cannot pass through

Index

24